MY SAVIOR FIRST OF ALL

Songs of Heaven's Promise

Arranged for Solo Piano
By Cindy Berry

Lillenas PUBLISHING COMPANY
Kansas City, MO 64141

My Savior First of All

CONTENTS

My Savior First of All

JOHN R. SWENEY
Arranged by Cindy Berry

He Hideth My Soul

WILLIAM J. KIRKPATRICK
Arranged by Cindy Berry

Tenderly ♩ = ca. 112

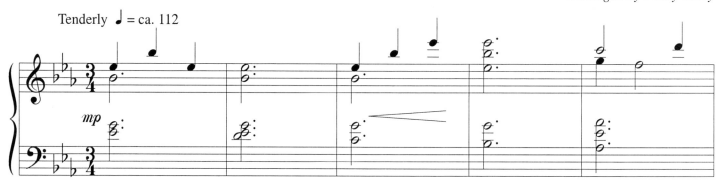

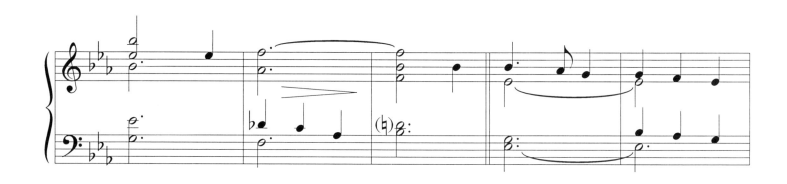

For All the Saints

RALPH VAUGHAN WILLIAMS
Arranged by Cindy Berry

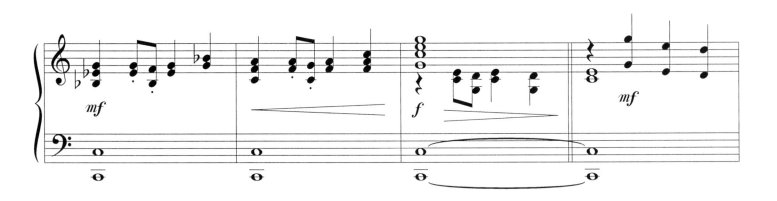

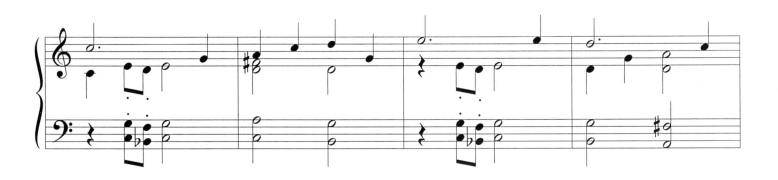

He the Pearly Gates Will Open

ELSIE AHLWEN
Arranged by Cindy Berry

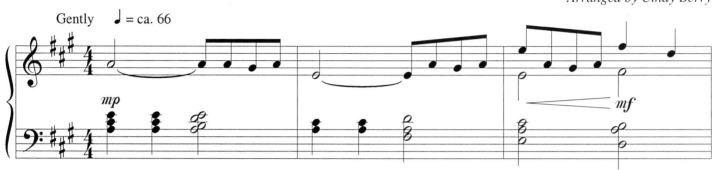

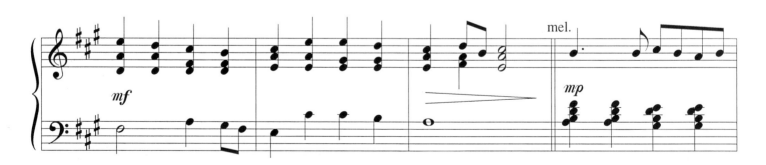

Glorious Things of Thee Are Spoken

FRANZ JOSEPH HAYDN
Arranged by Cindy Berry

Majestically, a little slower

For Carrie

My Jesus, I Love Thee

ADONIRAM J. GORDON
Arranged by Cindy Berry

With expression ♩ = ca. 76

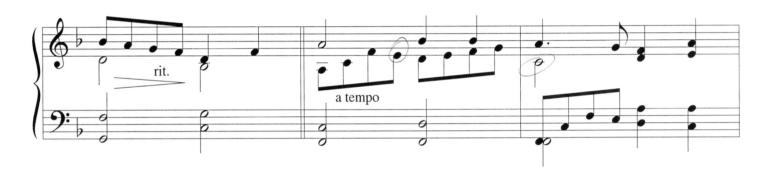

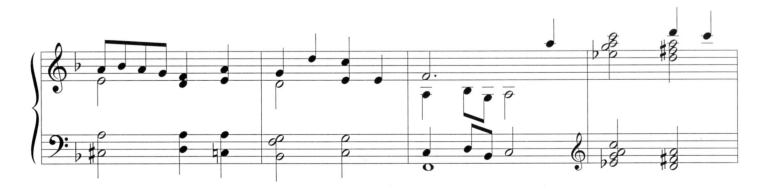

O That Will Be Glory

CHARLES H. GABRIEL
Arranged by Cindy Berry

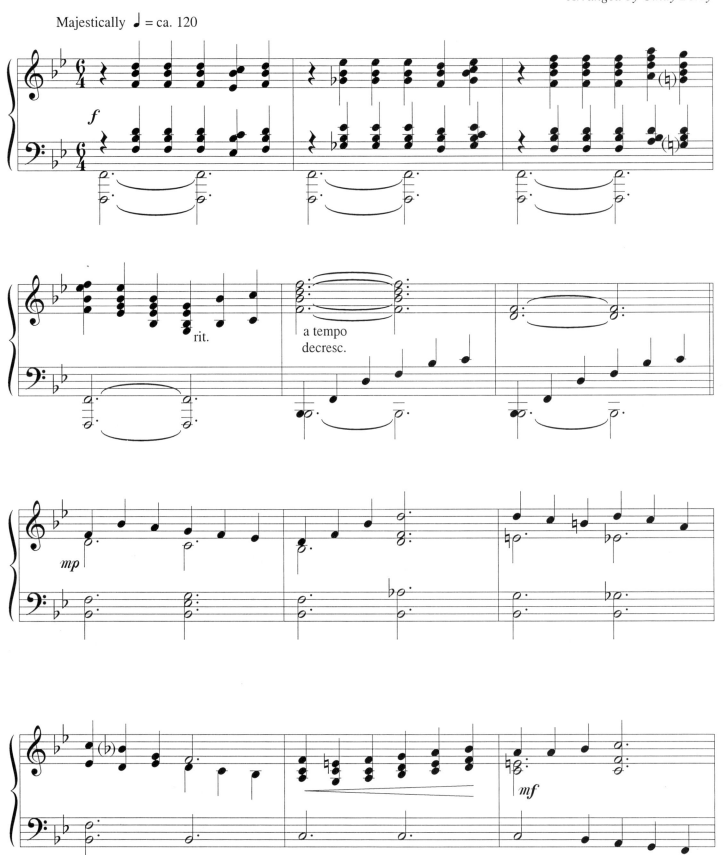

Ring the Bells of Heaven

GEORGE F. ROOT
Arranged by Cindy Berry

Joyfully ♩ = ca. 112

Saved by Grace

GEORGE C. STEBBINS
Arranged by Cindy Berry

With emotion ♩ = ca. 69

Sweet By-and-by

JOSEPH P. WEBSTER
Arranged by Cindy Berry

Soon and Very Soon

ANDRAE CROUCH
Arranged by Cindy Berry

With a gospel feel   ♩ = ca. 66

When We All Get to Heaven

EMILY D. WILSON
Arranged by Cindy Berry

In military style ♩ = ca. 116